# Sharing Success— Owning Failure

## Preparing to Command in the Twenty-First Century Air Force

DAVID L. GOLDFEIN
Colonel, USAF

Air University Press
Maxwell Air Force Base, Alabama

October 2001

**Disclaimer**

Opinions, conclusions, and recommendations expressed or implied within are solely those of the author and do not necessarily represent the views of Air University, the United States Air Force, the Department of Defense, or any other US government agency. Cleared for public release: distribution unlimited.

# *Contents*

# *Foreword*

Command is the ultimate service. It is a time when we have the singular responsibility to create and lead strong Air Force units. A time when our passion for our Air Force and our vision for its future must be overwhelmingly clear.

Early in the "Developing Aerospace Leaders" initiative, we began to focus on the way in which the institution teaches leadership and prepares airmen for command. What we found was a wide range of practices and a wide range of expectations—a complicating factor in today's Expeditionary Aerospace Force.

We realize that preparing our officers to command effective, mission-oriented units must be a deliberate process. It must develop our unique airman perspective, creating commanders who are able to communicate the vision, have credibility in the mission area, and can lead our people with inspiration and heart.

The foundation of our institution's effectiveness has always been its leaders. Colonel Goldfein's work provides valuable lessons learned and serves as a worthwhile tool to optimize your effectiveness as a squadron commander.

This book is a must–read, not only for those selected to command a squadron but for all our young officers, helping them understand what the requirements of squadron command will be. Remember, command is a unique privilege—a demanding and crucial position in our Air Force.

*Sharing Success—Owning Failure* takes you a step closer to successfully meeting that challenge.

Charles D. Link
Major General, USAF, Retired

# *About the Author*

Colonel Goldfein with his fellow Aviano warriors during Operation Allied Force

Colonel Dave "Fingers" Goldfein entered active duty in 1983 following graduation from the USAF Academy. He has completed a Masters in Business Administration, Squadron Officer School, Air Command and Staff College, Air War College, and the State Department Senior Seminar.

Fingers earned his pilot wings at Sheppard AFB, Texas, in 1984 and remained there as a first assignment instructor pilot (FAIP) in the Euro-NATO Joint Jet Pilot Training Program. Following Sheppard, he checked out in the F-16 Fighting Falcon and joined the 17th Tactical Fighter Squadron at Shaw AFB, South Carolina. During this tour, the squadron deployed to Abu Dhabi, United Arab Emirates, where Fingers led his flight on 40 combat missions over Iraq during Operation Desert Storm.

Upon returning from the United Arab Emirates, Fingers was selected for Weapons School and reassigned as initial cadre to build the composite wing at Mountain Home AFB, Idaho. Flying with the 389th T-Bolts, Colonel Goldfein served as squadron weapons officer and then chief of wing weapons, tactics, and intelligence.

Following Air Command and Staff College in residence, Fingers served as Aide de Camp to the Commander of AIRSOUTH in Naples, Italy, and then as Executive Officer to the USAFE Commander at Ramstein AFB, Germany.

In 1997, Colonel Goldfein re-qualified in the F-16 and returned to Europe as Operations Officer and then Commander of the 555th Triple Nickel Fighter Squadron at Aviano AB, Italy. As commander, Fingers led his squadron on combat missions over Serbia, Kosovo, and Bosnia-Herzegovina during Operation Allied Force. He is a command pilot with over 3,500 flying hours. His decorations include the Distinguished Flying Cross (1 OLC), Defense Meritorious Service Medal, Meritorious Service Medal (1 OLC), and Air Medal (5 OLC).

For 18 years and 13 moves, Fingers has been married to Dawn (Thumbs). They are the proud parents of two daughters, Danielle and Diana. He currently serves as deputy chief of Combat Forces Division at Headquarters USAF, Pentagon.

# *Preface*

Congratulations on your selection for the most challenging and rewarding job in the Air Force—squadron command. The intent of this paper is to help you prepare mentally for the task ahead by discussing a few themes central to a successful command tour. It will not answer all of your questions about *"how to command";* nor will it break any radically new ground in the "*art of leadership.*" Rather, the ideas expressed here are intended to spark your imagination as you begin preparing now for how *you* want to command *your* squadron.

These thoughts are not mine alone. In researching this project, I asked officers from across the Air Force, recently from command, to share stories of the greatest challenges they faced. What was the environment? How did they react? Why did they choose a particular path? Most importantly—what did they learn from the experience? Many of the stories I included in this paper involve situations in which the individual failed. Why? Because it is from studying our failures that we learn, grow, and improve as officers and leaders. As a commander, you will be privileged to share in many successes of your organization; however, you will personally own every failure. In the end, this is the true *loneliness of command.* Failure comes with risk and both are integral to a successful command tour.

So read over the ideas presented here with a critical eye and think now about how you will react given similar circumstances. Ask important questions such as: What are my expectations of command? What do the troops expect of me? What will be my vision? How will I create an environment that ensures mission success? How will I build my team? How will I handle justice? Who is ultimately responsible for fun in my squadron? By thinking critically about these questions now, you will be better prepared to lead successfully in the greatest job you will ever have.

Good luck commander!

Dave "Fingers" Goldfein

# Acknowledgments

I am greatly indebted to the officers who participated in this project. Sharing *success* is relatively easy. Owning *failure*, however, and then sharing the story of that failure in a published paper takes courage and a commitment to helping you succeed. Additionally, this project was significantly improved by the keen insight and editing skill of Maj Gen Perry Smith, USAF, retired. His book, *Rules and Tools for Leaders*, remains among the most practical guides on command and leadership written.

Maj Gen L. D. Johnston

Maj Gen (retired) Chuck Link

Brig Gen Dan "Fig" Leaf

Col Daniel "Doc" Zoerb
Col Jim "Rev" Jones
Col Judy Fedder
Col Dave "Face" Nichols

Col Lansen Conley
Col Jeff "Weird" Harrell

Lt Col Bill "Bigfoot" Eliason
Lt Col Theresa "Junior" Giorlando
Maj Duane "Imus" Creamer
SMSgt Michael Brake
SMSgt Christopher Schloemer

Maj Gen (retired) Perry M. Smith

Maj Gen (retired) Bob Taylor

Brig Gen (sel) Steve "Goldy" Goldfein

Col Terry "Hubba" New
Col Charlie "Clyon" Lyon
Col Brian "Bbop" Bishop
Col Anthony "Tony" Rebello

Col Mike "Boe" Boera
Lt Col Jeff "Butkus" Lofgren

Lt Col "Ragman" Harvey
Lt Col Steve Laushine
SMSgt John Long
SMSgt Beverly Hill
MSgt Larry Johnson

*Sharing Success—Owning Failure: Preparing to Command in the Twenty-First Century* was originally written as a research report for the National Foreign Affairs Training Center, Arlington, Virginia.

The photographs in this volume portray Allied Forces personnel at Aviano Air Base, Italy, during Colonel Goldfein's tour of duty as squadron commander, 555th Fighter Squadron. All are USAF photographs.

# *Abstract*

The single most important element of success in war is leadership. Leaders inspire others to achieve "above and beyond." The expectations of both leader and follower play key roles in the development of leadership, as do the leader's vision, the working environment, and the example established by the leader. The squadron commander is essential to accomplishing the mission of the United States Air Force. He or she must ensure that justice prevails among and between those commanded, and he or she must establish programs that promote health and happiness among the families within the command.

# Chapter 1

# **Expectations of Command**

> *Excellent leaders stand for absolute integrity, absolute honesty. They preach the concept of honesty in the organization. Excellent leaders practice integrity in thought, word, and deed. And they insist upon integrity and honesty on the part of their subordinates.*
>
> —Gen W. L. Creech, USAF, Retired

Any dialogue on preparation for command must begin with a discussion on expectations. No doubt you clearly remember the day you were informed that you had been chosen for command. Anticipation mixed with pride and a fair amount of uncertainty and fear—sound familiar? This section will discuss some key issues associated with what your boss expects, what your troops expect, and, perhaps most important, what you can expect.

# **What Does the Boss Expect?**

*As a wing commander, the most important personnel decision I ever made was the selection of my squadron commanders. No other officer would have a greater positive or negative effect on our ability to accomplish the mission.*

—Brig Gen Dan Leaf
31st Fighter Wing Commander

Leaders who hire subordinate commanders have a responsibility to clearly lay out their expectations for success. Too often, command in the Air Force is viewed as a test of the individual for future service rather than an opportunity for the organization to succeed and thrive under proven leadership. This over-arching focus on testing the *individual* rather than the success of the *unit* has resulted over time in a correspondingly shallow program to formally prepare you for command.

A Navy officer who is chosen for a 36-month command tour will spend the first 18 months as executive officer (focused on learning the art of command) in the very unit he or she will eventually lead. An

Army or Marine officer will attend several long training courses focused on command and leadership prior to accepting the colors of his or her first unit. In contrast, Air Force officers selected for command are currently required to attend a one-week major command (MAJCOM) squadron commander's course focused largely on *staying out of jail* rather than leading and managing effectively. This lack of emphasis on thoroughly preparing an individual to succeed in command suggests an even greater need for you and your new boss to establish mutually understood expectations for success.

As you begin the transition process, set up an appointment with your commander. Ask about his or her expectations and indicate that you are open to any advice—your commander has likely been in your position. Do not arrive without pen and pad in hand. One officer I know showed up for an interview with his numbered Air Force commander and was tossed out of the office to find writing tools—definitely not the way you want to begin your tour! The bottom line: Do not leave the interview until you understand clearly what is expected of you.

Sometimes, a face-to-face meeting is not possible prior to a command change. In these cases, send a note to your new boss and request his or her thoughts on success. Col William Lord, who served as communications director for Headquarters Air Mobility Command (HQ AMC), outlined his expectations in a letter to his new commanders. It helps them chart their own course for success:

Congratulations on being named squadron commander—it is the best job in the Air Force, and the toughest. To help you get off on the right foot, I'd like to offer some words to help with your mental preparation.

To start with, you need a command philosophy and initial focus. Three reasons: (1) you only have one chance at a first impression, (2) for much of what you actually accomplish in your 2-year command tour, you must first establish a focus in your initial 6 months, and (3) your first few weeks will haunt you if you aren't prepared. Those entrusted to your charge want and need to be led from day 1 of your command tour.

Get to know and network with your fellow commanders—irrespective of career field, MAJCOM, or specialty. If you succeed, you will become senior officers together before you know it. You will need one another. If you regard each other as competitors, you will hurt yourselves, your command chain, and our Air Force. Don't get lost in the "glamour of being the boss." You'll find the experience produces many rewards (not awards) along with a good measure of hard work and disappointments.

Now is a good time to send a short thank you to family members and any mentors that helped you during your career. Don't substitute with email [sic]—the personal touch and a hand-written [sic] note show good breeding. If you haven't sent a note to your new boss and wing king, do so—they selected you.

Take time to scrutinize your personal affairs. From relationships to money matters, you need to be squeaky clean. As a commander, you will sit in judgment of others, and you cannot afford to surrender the moral high ground—ever! You are expected to be above reproach. Your personal life won't get you promoted, but it can rapidly do you in.

Study up on your officers and senior NCOs before you take command—my office can help with personnel briefs and RIPs. These are your charges—worry about them, guide them, and develop them to become your replacement, or at least someone you'd be proud to have associated with your name. These troops shouldn't be worrying about their next assignment—that's your job.

Plan out your first 30 days now and have in mind what you want to accomplish. Some hints:

- Publish your command philosophy.

- Meet with your Top 3 (or 4) the first day.

- Visit every work center and every shift. Keep these visits regular.

- Determine the areas you are least comfortable with and focus on these. Don't be afraid to ask questions—the troops will respect your interest

- Meet all of your fellow commanders on their turf.

- Call on the Wing SEA, MPF Flight Commander, Chaplain, and all other agencies that provide service to your unit.

- Inspect the dorm and eat in the dining facility.

- Write job descriptions of each of your key subordinates and give them out one on one.

- Schedule a commander's call within the first month.

Take ownership of every part of your organization and teach this to subordinate leaders. Once you've walked past trash on the ground, a wall that needs paint, or a broken door, you've just blessed it—and you'll continue to overlook it every day after that—until it gets pointed out by your boss.

Establish immediately that your signed signature is your bond. It's hard to get credibility back once your name becomes meaningless. Always insist on putting the actual date of signature on everything you sign.

Spouse involvement in unit and base activities—there aren't any absolutes. The only wrong answers are zero and everything. If your spouse is a joiner and a doer, encourage it. If not—don't force it. Just remember that taking care of the families in your unit is an important part of the job—we recruit individuals, but we retain families. How you go about this will vary but the responsibility will always exist. If not your spouse, find someone who will help you lead in this area.

Finally, be an officer and an airman first—a communicator last. Aerospace power is our business—command information is our contribution. Make a concerted effort to stay current on operational issues and doctrine. If you don't understand aerospace power application, it's nearly impossible to effectively support the business.

Again, congratulations on your selection for command. I look forward to working with you to accomplish our mission.[1]

Are there any questions as to what this leader expects of his new commanders? With a few personal touches, this letter can serve as an excellent start for your letter to subordinate leaders and supervisors. Remember, establishing clear and mutually understood expectations with your flight commanders and flight chiefs will be your responsibility as commander.

## What Do the Troops Expect?

*Good leaders are people who have a passion to succeed . . . To become successful leaders, we must first learn that no matter how good the technology or how shiny the equipment, people-to-people relations get things done in our organizations. People are the assets that determine our success or failure.*

—Gen Ronald R. Fogleman, USAF, Retired

Now what about the troops—what are their expectations of you as a new commander? To answer this question, I surveyed the USAF Senior Noncommissioned Officer (NCO) Academy at Maxwell Air Force Base (AFB)–Gunter Annex, Alabama, and asked attendees to answer the following questions:

- What do you expect from your new commander?

- How do you define a successful commander?

- What do you not want to see in your new boss?

Among the most thoughtful responses came this one from SMSgt Michael Brake, a flight leader at the academy and former assistant to commander in chief strategic command (CINCSTRATCOM):

1. I expect leadership in action—not by proxy. Commanders must get out from behind their own perceived comfort zones and get to know their folks. I've experienced too many stories of shift personnel being surprised by senior leadership visiting them on a mid, swing,

or weekend shift. Shouldn't be a surprise—should be expected. No other way for the commander to get the true pulse of their personnel.

2. Leaders make mistakes—and grow through the opportunity. Don't be afraid to make them and fess up when you do—subordinates will know you are real. At the same time, understand that subordinates also make mistakes and need the same opportunity to grow as a result. Accountability yes, perfection—impossible.

3. Communication is vital—goes with number 1. Unless it is detrimental to the organization, share information. The result will be inclusion and fewer rumors, thereby making everyone feel significant.

4. Empower personnel. Former Chief Master Sergeant of the Air Force Sam Parrish said it best: "If what they want to do is (a) good for the Air Force; (b) good for the individual; and (c) doesn't hurt anyone—why stop them?

5. Live by the core values. Live by the core values. Live by the core values.[2]

Here is another entry from SMSgt Beverly Hill, also a flight chief at the Senior NCO Academy and former command systems manager at Robins AFB, Georgia, who explains her expectations of a new commander as follows:

1. In the commander, I am looking for someone who lives the core values every day. If you are wrong, admit it up front. Have the courage to stand up, without ever compromising personal beliefs, for what is right and fair. Don't say one thing and do another—we see what is *done,* not what is *said.*

2. I define a successful commander as one who supports, and in some cases stands up, for his or her people when they are right. Additionally, I look for someone who treats everyone fairly and is inclusive (decision makers should include male, female, minorities, enlisted). Finally, a successful commander has high standards

and demands that his/her officers also reflect and live the core values.

3. What I don't want to see is a commander who is partial to certain individuals; one who won't support you as a professional; or one who doesn't have the courage to support tough, unpopular decisions up the chain of command. Clearly, I don't want a commander who is dishonest.[3]

The final entry comes from SMSgt Christopher Schloemer, former first sergeant and now an instructor at the Senior NCO Academy:

1. Listen. I have a lot of experience to offer. Nothing puts me off more than a new commander that knows it all already. Obviously, you have new ideas and a new perspective, but hopefully, also an open mind.

2. Be decisive. A wishy-washy commander is death for an organization. Make informed decisions as much as possible. See #1 above.

3. Be consistent. As with anyone, you will have both good days and bad. However, if the troops come in and ask the secretary "what kind of mood is he/she in today," your organization will not be as effective.

4. Be visible. The troops need to see you. I used to put "walk around" time on my commander's schedule. Nothing raises morale more than knowing the commander cares enough to visit them in their work areas.

5. Don't micromanage. You don't have time to handle every detail. That's why you have so many people in your squadron.

6. Have high expectations of your senior NCOs. Hold their feet to the fire and ensure they are earning the title "senior NCO" every day by upholding high standards and leading troops.

7. Integrate the core values into your squadron every day. If you expect your troops to live by these, you

must live by them. I once had a commander who made reference to the core values in every corrective action he took—it was very effective.[4]

If there is a central theme in all of the essays I received, it is the expectation that commanders live the core values every day. While accomplishing this might appear simple, it takes continuous effort to ensure you never make a decision or take action that might give the impression (even unintentionally) that you are compromising these core values.

As an example, here is a story of a bad decision I made while commander of the 555th Fighter Squadron. It taught me a great deal about unintentional consequences.

The time and place: July 1999 at Aviano Air Base (AB), Italy

We had recently ended Operation ALLIED FORCE, the air campaign over Serbia and Kosovo. I received a call from aviation artist Robert Taylor, among the most respected and well-known painters of military aircraft in the world, asking for assistance. He was working on a painting of the F-16 entitled "Viper Venom" and asked for help by providing unclassified information on our squadron aircraft. Talking on the phone to the artist, we worked together to ensure he had the exact details in order to recreate the F-16 to his impeccable standards. Shortly after the painting was completed, I received a call from his staff asking if I would agree to sign the print as a commander and combat veteran (all of his aircraft paintings are signed). I was both honored and humbled by the request. After some thought and discussion with the JAG to ensure there was no ethical or legal dilemma, I agreed to sign the print. Additionally, I shared the story of a particular mission that highlighted the international NATO team effort of ALLIED FORCE. So why was this a failure?

First—as a commander, I failed to put my troops first. Remember what Colonel Lord said in his letter? There are rewards that come with command—not awards. By allowing myself to be singled out, I failed to represent my people, who contributed more than I ever did. A commander should be out front and in the lead in all but one circumstance—when there are accolades to be received or success to be shared.

Second—I failed my fellow commanders who fought side by side with me. A commander has loyalty to three groups—his command chain, his fellow commanders, and those he is privileged to lead. By not insisting that my fellow commanders be represented on the print, I failed to fight for their interests and the interest of their squadrons.

Finally, and most important for this discussion: when I had time to ponder this decision in the weeks and months that followed, I had to admit that I had not put service before self. In Senator John McCain's book, *Faith of My Fathers,* he states, "glory and honor are achieved only when one serves something greater than himself." The very best commanders are truly selfless in all things and at all times.

This was a great lesson on making decisions with our USAF core values in focus. While your initial intentions may very well be honorable, you must think through your decisions and actions to ensure our Air Force core values are at the heart of your existence every hour of every day.

## What Do You Expect?

*A good leader sets goals, measures progress, and rewards perform-ance. He or she tries to give every-one a stake in the mission of the organization and its outcome. That's the role of leadership.*

—Gen John M. Loh, USAF, Retired

To complete our discussion on expec-tations, we must explore perhaps the most difficult question to answer—what should you expect from the command experience? A squadron command tour is equal parts inspiration and aggrava-tion—times of exhilaration and times of depression. It is all-encompassing, and it becomes pervasive in every aspect of your life. Decisions will often be gut-wrenching and unclear. Your people will, at times, both inspire you and disappoint you. It will be, for many, the first time you are responsible for areas you don't truly understand; that is, outside your technical stovepipe and/or comfort zone. The larger and more diverse the organization under your command, the greater this discomfort will be.

As a new commander, you might be hesitant to ask questions of subordinates for fear of appearing uninformed and losing respect. Remember, however, that you have been chosen for command because of your demonstrated leadership abilities. You will garner far more respect from your airmen if you take the time early in your tour to understand their part in achieving your vision. Can you think of a single instance during your career when a commander asked you to explain what you do or how you do it and you were bothered by the intrusion? Chances are, you appreciated the fact that he or she took the time to ask your opinion. Your airmen will be no different. They don't expect immediate tactical or technical expertise in every area. However, they do expect you to understand how they fit into the big picture so you can be a credible advocate.

Maj Gen John G. Meyer, USA, wrote an outstanding book titled *Company Command: The Bottom Line.* (You need a copy!) General Meyer asks the following key questions, aptly describing the command experience:

1. Are you willing to dedicate yourself 24 hours a day, seven days a week, if necessary, for your unit and your troops?

2. Is your family willing to bear the sacrifices?

3. Are you willing to lead by example in everything you do—to live in a fish bowl with your personal and professional life open to view?

4. Do you understand that loyalty is a two-way street?

5. Can you challenge your troops to go the extra mile, knowing the challenges may increase even though the rewards remain the same?

6. Are you willing to put your neck on the line and take risks when necessary?

7. Are you willing to make the tough decisions, regardless of the consequences?

8. Are you willing to take responsibility for everything that happens, or doesn't happen, in your unit?

9. Are you willing to support your boss completely and wholeheartedly, even if he or she is not a person you like?

10. Are you willing to sacrifice your career to protect and preserve the dignity of your troops?[5]

If your answer to each of these questions is "yes," then you can expect to enjoy the single most difficult, most challenging, and most rewarding professional experience of your career.

In the next chapter, I will offer some thoughts on the commander's vision and share a few stories intended to help you develop and communicate your own vision. I will then offer some ideas on building an environment for success.

## **Notes**

1. Col William T. Lord, USAF, interviewed by author, November 2000.

2. SMSgt Michael Brake, USAF, interviewed by author, December 2000.

3. SMSgt Beverly Hill, USAF, interviewed by author, January 2001.

4. SMSgt Christopher Schloemer, USAF, interviewed by author, January 2001.

5. John G. Meyer, Maj Gen, *Company Command: The Bottom Line* (Washington, D.C.: National Defense University Press, 1990), 8. Reprinted with permission by Byrrd Enterprises, Inc., Alexandria, Va., 1996.

# Chapter 2

# **Vision and Environment**

*In the end, commanders do only two things—provide the vision and set the environment. Almost everything you do for the organization falls into one of these categories. You will be tempted to focus elsewhere. If you do so, it is likely you are performing someone else's job and they neither want nor need your help.*

—Col Steve Goldfein
1st Fighter Wing Commander

You were not hired to "tread water" in command. Rather, you are expected to move your squadron in a direction that more effectively accomplishes the unit's mission. This is true regardless of whether you are taking charge of a top-notch squadron or one that's on its back. Even the very best organizations can and will improve under the leadership of an inspirational commander. Developing a clear vision and then communicating that vision effectively are essential elements of successful command.

# Developing and Communicating Your Vision

*I am interested in the future because that's where I plan to spend the rest of my life.*

—Maj Gen Perry Smith, USAF, Retired

Add one year from your change of command day and ask yourself where you want the squadron to be. What specific goals do you want the squadron to achieve? Take the time to put these thoughts down on paper. You will find this exercise to be extremely useful for organizing your thoughts into a coordinated plan and a focused effort. This list becomes the foundation of your commander's intent—your vision. How you intend to accomplish these goals is not critical at this point.

The next step is to combine this list of goals into a basic *vision statement*. Remember that your airmen want, need, and deserve to be led from day one of your command tour. Knowing the direction their commander wants to take them is both comforting and reassuring. Here are some basic guidelines for developing your vision statement:

- Make it *understandable*—It must be understood by the entire squadron. Ensure that it is clear, concise, and easy to remember.

- Make it *inclusive*—Look over every aspect of your squadron and ensure that no section is left out of your vision.

- Make it *supportive*—Remember that your squadron is responsible for executing a portion of the wing's mission. Your vision must support the group and wing.

- Encourage *participation*—Avoid the tendency to "issue" your vision. Allow senior supervisors to make comments and tweak the vision statement before it is published. Their buy-in will flow down through the unit and help it to take solid root.

Here are two examples of vision statements to help you develop your own:

- When my brother, Col Steve Goldfein, stood up an AEF at Kwang Ju, he had airmen assigned from ten different PACAF bases with people going in as many directions. To get everyone aligned, he developed the following five-phase program: reception and beddown, force security, C3, mission continuation, and leaving the place better than we find it—do one before moving to the next. Simple, understandable, and everyone understood their role.

- My predecessor in command, Lt Col Guy Dahlbeck, had done a marvelous job transforming the squadron from a relatively new unit into a showplace for the wing. I determined that my role was to build on his excellent work and focus on rapid mobility in keeping with the move to an Expeditionary Air Force. Our vision became "arrive on time, with the right tools, the right training, and the right attitude to get the job done right the first time – Nickel standard." Again—catchy, inclusive, and easy to remember.

A final thought on developing your vision: Do not wait until after you have taken the unit colors to accomplish this critical task. Think about it right now. Make out your list of goals; talk it over with your peers. Use the time available between learning of your command assignment and taking command to think through this process. Like elected officials, you will experience a "honeymoon period" during which your troops will gauge you as their new leader. You must not squander the opportunity to lead from the beginning of your tour with a clear sense of direction and purpose. I will repeat a previous statement because it is so critical to successful command: *Your troops want, need, and deserve to be led from day one of your command tour.*

Once you have developed your vision, you must then communicate it throughout the squadron. Take and make every opportunity to talk to your troops about your vision and their role in it. It should become the centerpiece of a "mini-speech" you give when meeting with members of the squadron. Repetition in the early months of your command is critical to ensuring that the word filters to all levels of the organization. When Ronald W. Reagan was president, he stuck to a few key themes throughout his eight years in office. As he constantly repeated these ideas, we came to understand more clearly the direction he intended to lead our nation. On a slightly smaller scale, you must do the same as commander of your squadron. By taking the time to first develop and then communicate your vision to the squadron, you will begin your command tour with a clear sense of direction and purpose. The next step is to build the environment in the squadron to achieve your vision.

# **Building the Environment**

*Learn from the mistakes of others. You won't live long enough to make them all yourself.*

—Martin Fanbee

Every day, more than 95 percent of your airmen will arrive at work intending to succeed—very few come in intending to fail. Your role as commander is to build an environment within the squadron with as few barriers as possible to achieving this already sought-after success. The work area must be secure, safe, of high standard, and respectful of diversity.

The most challenging aspect of building this environment will be establishing open and engaged communication flow within the unit. As the commander, you set the tone for the entire squadron. Are you an *active* and *engaged* listener? Do you maintain eye contact when people are talking? Do you ask questions to clarify their positions? Do you encourage diversity of opinions on issues? Can you summarize a complex discussion into logical points at the end of a staff meeting? All of these are essential characteristics of an active listener. Not only must you set the example as the commander; you must mentor your key supervisors to do the same. After you have given direction in a staff meeting, wait a few days and then ask a few airmen if they have heard the guidance. You'll often be disappointed in what you find. Go back to the top and start again. It takes constant vigilance throughout your command tour to keep information and ideas flowing daily in all directions. In almost every case study presented in this paper, as well as virtually every mishap board you will ever be involved in, a breakdown in communication at some point is causal. Work at improving communication every day until you give up command.

You can use (or develop, if required) a few key organizations within your squadron to assist in facilitating communication flow. Four such key organizations are discussed below.

1. *Flight Commander Forum*—Most squadrons are organized such that every airman is assigned to one of your flight commanders. Establish a forum with just you and your subordinate commanders to discuss issues related to the squadron. Meet once a month and use the opportunity to share your thoughts as well as prepare them for future leadership responsibility.

2. *Top 3 (or 4)*—Meet with your senior NCOs within the first few days of taking command. Establish clearly that you intend to meet with them on a regular basis to discuss issues facing the squadron. Again, work to get their participation and recruit them to help communicate your vision and intent to the troops.

3. *Airman's Advisory Council*—This is a superb forum for offering younger airmen the opportunity to raise

issues directly with the commander as well as hear from you. Not only work to get their commitment to supporting your vision, also use the forum to check communication flow throughout the squadron. Did your direction at the last staff meeting make it out? Ask and see.

4. *Spouse Support Group*—Our families exhibit a special kind of courage when they endure the long hours, the separations, and the hardships so common to our service. We owe it to these unsung heroes to ensure they are informed about squadron activities and to make them feel part of the unit's mission. Share your vision with them—they deserve to know and you want their involvement.

Here is a story from Lt Col Jeff Lofgren, commander of an F-16 Fighter Squadron, that highlights a lesson he shares about listening to key supervisors:

The time and place: May 1999, Misawa AB, Japan

We had just returned from a deployment to the desert and were facing a
PACAF inspection in two months. The
orderly room had not deployed and
was expected to have completed all
inspection preparation while we were
gone—this had not happened. I called
a meeting to discuss orderly room
issues and to review where we were in
preparation for the upcoming inspection. At the end of the discussion, one
of the SSgts brought up the fact that
he was conducting ERGO testing and
requested to be allowed to return to
work in the squadron in athletic gear
since he was driving back and forth a
great deal (15 minutes each way). I
asked the NCOIC of the orderly room
his opinion. He was taken aback by
the question but responded that it
would in fact help if the SSgt could
come back to the squadron. I then
asked if anyone had brought up the
uniform attire as an issue. My first
sergeant said the chief had com-
mented on the fact that the SSgt had
been in the squadron in workout
attire. I did NOT listen very well at this
point. My shirt said he had already

spoken with the NCOIC and resolved the issue—he was hinting big and I wasn't listening! I was running late so I made a hasty decision I thought was no big deal and authorized the SSgt to wear athletic gear while accomplishing ERGO testing. Big mistake.

Later that afternoon my shirt came into my office and shut the door. Being the ultimate professional, he asked "may I speak frankly with you sir? You really messed up this morning." Right then all the subtle comments became clear. He proceeded to tell me that my chief had already resolved the issue by directing the shirt to instruct the NCOIC that the SSgt would not be allowed to wear athletic gear in the squadron. After discussing the issue with the NCOIC, the matter appeared closed. The SSgts felt they had won a small victory by undermining the authority of the senior NCOs.

My lessons were very clear. When your senior NCOs speak, you need to listen to them first and foremost. When the shirt mentioned that the chief had spoken on the issue, bells should have gone off. Next, my shirt had already handled the issue, told me so, and I trumped him—not a good thing to undermine his authority in front of subordinates. As a commander, you must listen to your senior NCOs, who are central to good order and discipline within your unit. This seemingly small issue turned out to haunt me for many months until I could reorganize the orderly room.[1]

Effective team building is another key to building a successful work environment. There are certain key relationships both within and outside your squadron that you must develop as a commander. The first I will discuss is the relationship between you and your senior enlisted leader, normally a chief master sergeant. As the senior enlisted manager, your chief is the main spokesman on all issues pertaining to the enlisted force. You must talk openly and often. As a young commander, you may feel a bit intimidated by a chief with 18-23 years in the service. Remember, however, in the end it is *your* squadron. You have several years of solid experience in the Air Force yourself, and it is what you do today with the experience you have that matters.[2] Never forget that the leadership skills you have developed up to this point in your career (which impressed your boss enough to hire you for command) are not tribe or specialty specific. The basics of solid leadership you used to motivate and lead officers as a flight commander will now apply to leading airmen (and visa versa).

Developing the right relationship with your chief is crucial to your success. Make it a point to never sign any paper associated with an enlisted issue before the chief gets a vote. Walk around the squadron with your chief so the troops see you together often. Listen to his/her advice. It will benefit you and your squadron if the troops know the chief has your ear and is a respected advisor. Think of the relationship as much like that of a father and son. To succeed, you must be mature enough to realize that while you are often the father, sometimes you are the son.[3]

The next relationship you must develop is between your first sergeant "shirt" and the chief. Often the lines of responsibility between these two individuals will cross and become clouded. It is essential that you lay out your expectations early so that these key advisors are in sync and in support of your vision. As a general rule, the shirt will be your primary advisor when you are working a discipline or personnel issue involving other base agencies (JAG, Family Support, etc.). However, no action should be taken with an airman in the squadron before the chief gets an input. On the other hand, when there are mission-related issues taking place with the enlisted force, the chief will be your primary advisor. Once again, the shirt must be *in the know* to ensure that he/she is not blindsided when counseling members of the squadron. It is all about *communication*. These two individuals must communicate openly and daily to ensure that neither works against the other and both work together for you. By laying out these expectations to them early, you will begin your tour with a solid base of senior NCO support and teamwork.

The final inside-the-squadron key team discussed here is the one between key supervisory officers who, by nature of your mission, will have conflicting interests. I'll use a typical fighter squadron as an example to discuss the relationship between the operations officer and the maintenance officer. The operations officer is responsible for training the pilots/aircrew while the maintenance officer is responsible for managing the fleet of aircraft and equipment. To build a healthy team spirit in these officers, who often have conflicting requirements, lay out your expectations to the two of them clearly. The operations officer has a responsibility to the maintenance officer to clearly explain the *value* of whatever it is he is asking for. This is important because the maintenance officer will have to explain any proposed plan to his staff.

The maintenance officer owes the operations officer the *cost* of what he is asking in terms of workload and impact on the long-term health of the fleet. The operations officer needs to understand this cost in order to educate his staff. Once both the *value* and the *cost* are clearly understood by both sides, reasonable men and women can reach informed decisions that balance each competing interest while accomplishing the mission. The key ingredient for success is engaged interaction and open communication by both sides.

When the operations officer and the maintenance officer cannot agree, you must make the decision. Before you do, bring them in and have them explain to you (and to each other) the value and cost as indicated above. You will likely find that a few sessions with you going through this process will help them communicate more effectively. This process can be applied to any squadron where equipment and facilities issues run counter to training agendas. It is useful to remember in these situations that each member of the squadron is after the same end state; that is, effective accomplishment of the squadron's mission. Disagreements generally center on the best method to get to this common goal.

The most critical team you must develop outside your squadron is between you and your fellow squadron commanders. Make appointments in the first few weeks to visit them on their turf. Get to know the civil engineering commander before you have to ask for her help. Remember Colonel Lord's advice in his letter about viewing your fellow commanders as "the competition." Do not let healthy competition turn into open animosity. As commander, you will set the tone. *Never* degrade or criticize other squadrons—to do so is to violate your loyalty to fellow commanders. Remember that weak organizations need another unit, usually a better one, to define who they are and what they stand for as a squadron. Define who you are internally rather than externally. Yours may well become the squadron other units will emulate.

Here is a superb story from Lt Col Jim Jones, commander of an F-16 Fighter squadron at Osan AB, Republic of Korea, that highlights teambuilding, listening, and building key relationships:

The time and place: June 1999, Osan AB, Republic of Korea

As I stood in front of the squadron during my change of command ceremony, I was confident I was as prepared to command as any officer could expect to be. I had extensive flying experience in the aircraft and had spent the previous thirteen months as the operations officer of the same squadron. I felt I had the big issues under control, but I quickly learned that some of the items I considered minor issues could have major repercussions.

When I took command, the maintenance personnel were operating on a three-shift concept. My maintenance supervisors were confident this was the most effective way to keep the fleet combat ready, plus it enabled them to stabilize the work schedules for personnel on the line. Instead of tying work schedules to the flying period, they were able to offer relatively stable work hours for our airmen, which was a significant quality of life issue. Sounded great in principle, but unfortunately, it was not in accordance with current regulations. As we were in the zone for a higher headquarters inspection, I had to decide whether we were going to continue with three-shift operations or realign the schedule to conform to PACAF's standard two-shift maintenance guidance.

I did some basic research on the regulation and then discussed the issue with the PACAF/LG staff. They gave me a number of reasons why the three-shift operation was a bad idea: manning shortfalls, lack of supervision, tendency to pass work to the next shift, etc. While they acknowledged there were isolated situations that might require three shifts, they presented very convincing arguments that this wasn't the best way to accomplish maintenance on a routine basis. As I saw it, the issue seemed relatively simple. Could we maintain the aircraft in the same manner and accomplish the mission in accordance with the regulations, or did we truly need to maintain three-shift operations? I asked my maintenance supervisors and they indicated that we certainly could meet mission requirements with two shifts—but at a cost in efficiency and quality of life benefits. After some thought, I elected to stop the three-shift operation as a standard practice, while maintaining the option to flex when circumstances dictated the need to do so.

While I believe the decision was correct and I would make the same decision today, the *way* I handled the situation turned out to have negative repercussions. My maintenance supervisors were extremely talented, experienced, and capable. This wasn't a decision they had come to by chance. They were confident they were doing what was best for the squadron, and when I told them I had discussed this with PACAF, they felt I didn't trust their judgment. I failed to realize how important this issue was to them. As a result, I didn't get them involved in the decision process as I should have. Rather than going to the PACAF staff alone, I should have included my maintenance supervisors in the discussion. When they wanted to discuss my rationale for going to two-shift operations, I felt I knew all of the counter arguments so cut off the discussion with a curt, "because that is what the regs say we need to do." I should have spent more time listening and understanding my maintenance supervisor's concerns and then included them in the final decision. The result of all of this was a perception among my senior NCOs that *the boss didn't trust or value their opinion.* A perceived lack of trust can lead to all sorts of problems. Had I taken the time to treat this issue as a team-building exercise rather than a solo commander decision, we could have resolved the situation and emerged stronger as a squadron.[4]

Another area you must consider as you build an environment for success is how to create a safe working environment in an inherently unsafe business. We are airmen. Our ultimate job, as an Air Force, is to rapidly dominate the air and space over a defined geographical area in support of national security objectives. This often involves the precise and deliberate destruction of selected enemy targets and loss of life. Nothing about the job is inherently safe. Working next to running jet engines is not safe. Deploying into high threat areas is not safe. Securing an airfield in a high terrorist threat condition is not safe. Dodging surface-to-air missiles is not safe. So how do you build a safe working environment under these conditions? One answer is by stressing *discipline*. A disciplined squadron will always be a safe squadron; however, the reverse is not necessarily true. Discipline to an aviator means strict adherence to the rules of engagement in war and to training rules in peacetime. Discipline to a maintainer means adherence to technical orders and precise documentation of work performed. A disciplined squadron will take pride in its facilities and work areas. Standards for wear of the uniform and personal appearance will be strict, understood, and supported by your supervision. Punish breaches of discipline immediately and openly. When you build your squadron safety program, focus on *discipline first*. Achieve it and you will be the safest operation on base with no sacrifice in mission readiness.

The last thought on building an environment for success involves developing a "*winning spirit*"—a general recognition that your squadron is up to the task despite the mission or level of competition. This is not something that happens overnight, but it can happen surprisingly quickly. A new commander at Shaw AFB took over a unit that had not won a single award in the two years previous to his change of command. He began with his senior staff focusing on winning the quarterly foreign object damage (FOD) award. Once they accomplished this task, they moved on to others, always focused on *team* rather than *individual* accomplishment. In the course of one year, the squadron was winning every competition on base. Morale soared as airmen recognized they were part of a winning team. It took a focused effort and diligence on the part of the commander to nurture this spirit in a way that still balanced his loyalty to both his fellow commanders and the airmen in his squadron.

While building an environment for success, you will not win every competition and you will not accomplish every task with perfection. There will be times when you will fall short both individually and as a unit. The best advice for handling not only setbacks but also achievement comes from Don Shula, the "winningest" coach in national football league (NFL) history. Coach Shula had a 24-hour rule. He allowed himself, his coaches, and his players a maximum of 24 hours to celebrate a victory or bemoan a defeat. Once the 24 hours was up, they put it behind them and focused their energies on the next opponent.[5]

Developing your vision, communicating your vision, and building an environment for success should take up the majority of your time and energy as a commander.

### Notes

1. Lt Col Jeff Lofgren, interviewed by author, February 2001.

2. John G. Meyer, *Company Command: The Bottom Line* (Washington, D.C.: National Defense University Press, 1990), 31. Reprinted with per-

mission by Byrrd Enterprises, Inc., Alexandria, Va., 1996.

3. Col Steve Goldfein, USAF, interviewed by author, January 1998.

4. Lt Col Jim Jones, USAF, interviewed by author, February 2001.

5. Kenneth H. Blanchard, *The Heart of a Leader* (Tulsa, Okla.: Honor Books, 1999), 19.

# Chapter 3

# **Walking the Walk**

*Leaders have the ability to inspire others to achieve what managers say is not feasible.*

—Gen Colin Powell, USA, Retired
Secretary of State

A great deal has been written about leadership and management and the difference between the two. I am going to use an oversimplified definition that should be useful for our discussion of command: *Leadership is about people; management is about things.* Successful commanders understand they are equally responsible for both. As a commander, you will be entrusted with both people and things (aircraft, vehicles, parts). You must balance your time between these areas of responsibility. Commanders who feel they can simply focus on leadership and not sweat the details of management have never seen what goes into the phase inspection of an aircraft or managed the supply requirements to keep a fleet of aging vehicles running in a transportation squadron. Commanders who believe they can focus just on managing the pieces and parts have never choreographed and led 100 aircraft into a heavily defended enemy target or made a gut-wrenching decision to relieve an incompetent subordinate. The bottom line is this: A successful commander balances his time between leadership and management responsibilities.

As a manager, you must get down deep enough into the organization to understand the key processes required to accomplish the mission. How can you engage to solve a supply problem if you don't understand how your people do their jobs? Don't believe you are *empowering* your people and avoiding micromanagement by *neglecting* to understand what is required (both integral to the squadron and outside) for your squadron to accomplish its mission. A blind and/or ignorant eye is not the same as empowerment.

As a leader, you must inspire your people to accomplish more than management rules would suggest is possible. You, along with every other commander in the USAF, will have fewer than the optimum number of personnel and resources needed to accomplish your mission—that is a fact of life. Understand clearly that these limitations do not constitute an excuse for failure to answer the call. Your inspirational leadership is required to overcome these and other obstacles in achieving mission success. Doing *more with less* is a fact of existence in the Air Force. Your challenge as a commander is to do the *very best you can with what you have.*

Here are several stories from commanders who faced daunting challenges during their tours. Read them with a critical eye and think now about how you might handle similar circumstances in the future.

The first involves a situation where the fundamental ethics of a commander were tested. This tale comes from Col Terry New.

The time and place: December 1993, Aviano AB, Italy

When I was commander of the 512th Fighter Squadron stationed at Ramstein AB, Germany, we deployed to Aviano for the 86th Wing's first participation in Operation DENY FLIGHT. The ground war in Bosnia was fairly intense at that point and escalating, with all sides trying to get their last licks in before winter. NATO airpower was providing 24-hour coverage over Bosnia, not only denying flight, but also providing a deterrent close air support presence for UN forces on the ground trying to mediate the conflict.

I led the deployment sortie to Aviano, where the 31st Wing Commander and staff gave us a warm reception. There was a lot of media coverage, including an interview as soon as my feet hit the ground. After a fair amount of gripping and grinning, I was invited to attend the wing standup where I was welcomed as one of their own. Up to this point, I was riding pretty high—first deployment as a squadron commander, about to fly the squadron's first combat missions, and a grand welcome by the 31st Fighter Wing. But when I returned to the squadron facility, my operations officer was waiting for me outside. "Boss, we need to talk. We've got a problem."

He had led the [advanced echelon] ADVON team down a few days prior and this was my first opportunity to talk with him since arrival. We had planned to load 500-lb Mark 82 bombs for the following day's schedule and expected a fuse that my weapons troops were certified to load. Problem was, these fuses did not exist at Aviano. So here we were, deployed for combat operations and not certified to load our primary air-to-ground munitions. The leadership at the Combined Air Operations Center (CAOC) in Vicenza was furious and demanded that we "do whatever it takes" to fly our tasking the next day.

We found my maintenance supervisor on the flight line and discussed options. He gave me an "out" by saying that although the weapons loaders were not certified to load the other fuses, they had done it before and would have no trouble doing it now for combat. They were leaning way forward and would do it if I gave the word. Those UN forces were depending on us to be overhead in case they needed help.

I tried to simplify the facts in my mind in order to make the right decision. Our site survey team had obviously done a poor job of determining the fuse inventory at Aviano. My "combat ready" squadron I was so proud of was not so "combat ready" and, in fact, we had egg all over our face. I had an O-6 at the CAOC speaking directly to the 2-star telling me to do "whatever it takes" to make our schedule the next day. And I had my maintenance supervisors, who felt bad about not discovering the fuse requirement, reassuring me they could load those bombs and fuses even though they were not certified to do so. All I had to do was give the word.

I thought back to my first commander's call and what I had said were my priorities as well as what I expected them to use as their priorities when making difficult decisions. Number one, ask yourself how this decision will affect our ability to do our mission. I had no doubt we could safely load the bombs and carry out combat operations the next day. But we'd be doing it in direct violation of Air Force Instructions. If anything went wrong, I wouldn't have a leg to stand on. Number two, ask yourself how this decision will affect our people. I felt they had already fulfilled their obligation by giving me an honest appraisal of where we stood. Any repercussions would be borne solely by me. It would probably even boost morale a bit for the troops to see the boss stick his neck out to preserve our squadron's reputation.

I felt I could justify a decision either way, based on my first two priorities. Number three, just do the right thing if you can't make the decision based on the first two priorities. So much for black and white decisions! All eyes were on me and they were waiting for a decision. Whatever I told them would demonstrate how I expected them to conduct themselves, not only as a member of the squadron, but throughout their Air Force careers. It suddenly became clear to me what to do.

I told them we were not going to load the bombs without certified loaders. We rolled up our sleeves and determined what it would take to get our loaders certified. I called my [operations group] OG back at Ramstein and told him what I had done and asked for help. He scrambled a C-21 with a certified weapons load crew and instructor on board and they were at Aviano in a matter of hours. He instructed and certified my weapons loaders while they loaded our first jet—legally. We met our tasking the next day and every day after that. My OG/CC and I jumped in a car and drove to the CAOC for an audience with the General and the Colonel. After tempers had calmed and we were flying combat missions, the general made his position very plain: "Don't let it happen again."

I've thought about this situation many times since then. I wouldn't do anything different. This event also has some leadership lessons at the next level of command because my commander saved my back end. He never once questioned my decision and went to extraordinary lengths to bail me out of a difficult situation. Once he brought the cavalry to the rescue, he could have jumped back on that C-21 and gone home. He chose instead to go with me to Vicenza to provide top cover and did most of the apologizing for me. Talk about how to win someone's respect—I'd work for him again any day![1]

This story also highlights an important part of making command decisions: learning to *trust your gut*. You have been placed in command because others already trust your instincts to make solid decisions. When you find yourself favoring a course of action because you think someone else might be smarter

than you, step back a moment. If your gut tells you it's wrong, don't go there. Many commanders at every level can tell plenty of stories of poor decisions they made that went against their gut instincts—and they knew it. Chances are, the longer you are in command, the more you will find these gut checks to be superb decision guides.

Lt Col Charlie Lyon, commander of the 22d Fighter Squadron at Spangdahlem, learned a lesson about paying attention to the details.

The time and place: March 1999, Spangdahlem AB, Germany

This was a great lesson for me in what happens if you don't check all the details as a commander. While the squadron was deployed to Incirlik, Turkey, in support of Operation Northern Watch (ONW), my life support officer was attending a school in the states. He returned to the squadron just before Operation Allied Force began.

We quickly redeployed the squadron to home station, finding out during our refueling stop at [Naval Air Station] NAS Sigonella that our destination was not Aviano but Spangdahlem, adding a new twist to our upcoming tasking: we would be flying out of home station with pilots who had not yet participated in Allied Force. Within 48 hours of arrival at Spangdahlem, we were airborne for our first Allied Force combat missions with a mix of pilots who had spent the previous months deployed to ONW and others who had remained at home station.

When we received the execute order, a certain young officer was included in the lineup. After his second mission, he was extremely shaken up—he had been launched on by enemy surface-to-air missiles on both missions. I learned from his flight commander that he was extremely hesitant to fly again the following night. Once I looked into the details, I found out this kid (who had only been mission ready for a couple of months) had only flown one or two night sorties TOTAL since being at Spangdahlem. So, we gave him a couple of simulator hops and rotated him to Aviano to fly daytime missions before working him back into the night rotation.

Looking back, this young pilot had more courage than the rest of us by flying in missions he hadn't been properly trained to do. Was he current and qualified to perform the mission? Yes. Was he the right choice to fly one of the missions early on? No. I let him down by placing him in a position he never should have been in—because I never checked the details.[2]

A critical aspect of successful command will be taking care of your troops. A story from Lt Col Mike Boera, commander of the 23d Fighter Squadron at Spangdahlem and former operations officer of the 22d, highlights the importance of putting this high on your priority list.

The time and place: December 1996, Karup, Denmark

I was lucky enough to learn a great lesson on leadership and taking care of my troops while serving as Operations Officer of the "Big 22" Fighter Squadron flying F-16s. I was the detachment commander for a tactical fighter weaponry deployment to Karup, Denmark. Our deployed maintenance team was already in place along with our advance team of operations personnel. As the deployment leader, I eagerly looked forward to this opportunity to get away from the office, the email [*sic*] terminal, and the headaches, to fly, learn, and have a great time. All the jets were down safely and I was met at the plane with a cold beer by one of the younger troops. I had an all-star team of performers with me, so I wasn't at all worried about being ready to go the next day. Time to have some fun.

Luckily, I had a superstar sortie generation element chief, SMSgt Ted Paget, who tactfully "let me have it." He pulled me aside on day two and told me I had messed up big-time by not checking on the troops first. I should have asked about the barracks. How is the chow? How is the transportation to and from the airfield? How are the maintenance facilities? Turns out they were all fine because I had a professional SNCO "checking my six" and ensuring the troops were cared for.

The first impression of me as a commander quite frankly stunk. Luckily, because of SMSgt Paget's timely guidance, I was able to rebound and become a better leader for the remainder of the deployment. Abraham Lincoln said, "I can make a general in five minutes, but it will take me years to come up with 100 good horses." As a commander, you better take care of the horses. I will never have to be reminded again.[3]

Unit failure is undoubtedly one of the most difficult situations for a commander to face. What do you do if the entire organization fails? Col Lansen Conley tells us about just such a situation he faced as a maintenance squadron commander.

The time and place: May 1996, Aviano AB, Italy

I commanded the 31st Maintenance Squadron (MXS) at Aviano AB, Italy. It was a large squadron of about 600 people responsible for several in-shop maintenance functions along with munitions storage and handling. For everyone in the munitions business, nuclear surety inspections (NSI) strike fear into the hearts of everyone involved. They are exacting inspections, requiring months of preparation and practice—failure is not an option.

For months prior to the NSI, we worked to ensure we were prepared—long hours, endless checks and rechecks. Thankfully, we passed the NSI. A month and a half later, [Headquarters USAF Europe] HQ USAFE scheduled us for a conventional munitions stockpile verification audit. When my boss, the logistics group commander, inquired about the nature of this audit, my munitions specialists said it was not graded and therefore low threat. Consequently, we did not spend a great deal of time preparing for the audit and I was assured we were ready. When the inspectors finished, we were labeled the "worst in USAFE"—a shock to everyone. Needless to say, the shock wave went all the way up the chain to HQ USAFE. It took months of endless hours to fix the problems and pass a re-inspection.

We had some serious mismanagement problems caused by failure to follow established procedures. I fired some supervisors, moved some to new positions, and hired a few new folks. Our young airmen had to work long and hard to correct deficiencies that didn't just occur overnight—it was a long-standing problem of bad practices and not following the book.

What did I learn from this? First, no inspection is benign. Never let your people tell you "not to worry" when higher headquarters inspection teams are in town.

Second, be the commander from Missouri with the "show me" approach. As one of my bosses would say, "trust but verify." This is especially true if the inspection is in an area where you don't have technical expertise. Ask all those "stupid" questions because while you are getting educated, it might trigger one of your experts in an area that needs to be checked. Invite experts in from another base, on your nickel, to get an outside opinion. We did this for the re-inspection and it paid big dividends.

Third, ensure that your senior supervisors know they are accountable. They need to know their areas cold. When they tell you they are ready for inspection, you expect them to be ready by the book—not according to how they "feel."

Fourth, if you get to stay on the job and fix the problem, be aggressive. Develop a get-well plan, complete with a timeline, and brief it up the chain. Figure out whom to hold accountable, and do so. Stay engaged and take the recovery on as a unit task.

Fifth and finally, always be the leader. Take responsibility for the failure and get out front of the recovery. Bad inspection results are no fun, but if you rally the squadron to overcome it as a unit, you will emerge stronger for it.[4]

As a commander, you must take your mission, but not yourself, very seriously. The final story in this section comes from Col Daniel "Doc" Zoerb, one of the most talented officers I have ever known. It offers some thoughts on the importance of *humility* as a commander:

The time and place: Early 1980s, Eglin AFB, Florida

There we were, forty-five of the USAF's very finest NCOs, hand-picked [*sic*] from throughout [tactical air command] TAC, two of the world's most gorgeous brand new air superiority fighters on alert with four outside, ready and waiting for the first opportunity to fight. The unit quickly becomes operational and is a political showplace—a model for tactical fighter employment and maintenance, a jewel in terms of facilities, and the first stop on any senior leader's or politician's tour. Young Captain Zoerb, in his first command, is approached by his old CMSgt one afternoon and asked for a minute of the commander's time behind closed doors. Into the commander's office they go, the chief carrying a glass of water. With the door closed, the chief, using his standard south Georgia drawl, asks the captain if he "would mind stickin' his fanger in this here glass of water." In a busy, condescending way, the captain agrees and puts a finger in the glass. The old chief takes a few seconds to inspect the water with the captain's finger stuck in it up to the knuckle, then asks him to remove the finger. The chief continues examining the glass of water and the now removed dripping finger, says, "hhruumphh . . . just what I thought," excuses himself, and leaves the office, never saying another word about the event . . . ever. Dismissing the event as rather strange, but of no significance, the commander struts out, gathers flying gear, and becomes the star of the day's practice scramble demonstration for a group of visiting State representatives.

0200 that night, out of a sound sleep, the meaning of the chief's strange behavior is realized: you court disaster when you start believing your own "stuff" or the "stuff" others are saying or writing about you or your organization.

There are a lot of reasons why organizations succeed or fail. Seldom is the intellect, experience, or leadership of a single individual the sole reason for either. It is dangerous to believe that a particular leadership style, or your particular characteristics, represents an infallible formula for success. Humility, recognition of the indispensable role played by each member of the team, flexibility/adaptability of leadership to current or anticipated environment, and an ability and a willingness to take advantage of new or fleeting opportunities make command a constant and dynamic challenge—and really hard work. We named our son Jacob after CMSgt (ret) Allison Jacobs . . . finest chief I ever knew.[5]

Clearly, this story highlights the notion that leaders with humility don't think less of themselves—they just think of themselves less.[6]

## Notes

1. Col Terry New, USAF, interviewed by author, February 2001.

2. Col Charlie Lyon, USAF, interviewed by author, January 2001.

3. Col (sel) Mike Boera, USAF, interviewed by author, January 2001.

4. Col Lansen Conley, USAF, interviewed by author, Dececmber 2000.

5. Col Daniel Zoerb, USAF, interviewed by author, November 2000.

6. Kenneth H. Blanchard, *The Heart of a Leader* (Tulsa, Okla.: Honor Books, 1999), 46.

# Chapter 4

# **Handling Justice**

*A leader must be able to look a man in the eye when he fires him and weep for him at the same time.*

—Vice Adm James Stockdale, USN, Retired

Much has been written about commanders and the *law* but relatively little has been written about commanders and *justice*. Guess which one you are ultimately responsible for? Because it will take up so much of your time as a commander and because getting it right is so critical to success, I have devoted an entire chapter to the process of handling justice in your squadron. What follows is not the "approved solution"; rather, it is a collection of thoughts on a process of justice for your consideration as you develop your own methods.

Military discipline, handled with fairness, timeliness, and compassion, is always positive. This is a very important statement, so I will repeat it: *Military discipline, handled with fairness, timeliness, and compassion, is always positive*. It may not feel very positive to the individual involved at the time, but when discipline is handled correctly, the squadron and the Air Force will benefit. Often, the individual will benefit as well. Discipline that is timely and fairly managed can significantly boost morale in a unit. Conversely, poorly managed discipline will severely undermine your credibility and your capacity to lead effectively.

When a subordinate in your squadron fails (or appears to fail) in the performance of his/her duties, take the time to ask yourself and the affected supervisors four key questions:

1. Did the individual have a clear understanding of the task?

2. Did the individual have the required tools?

3. Did the individual have the required training?

4. Did the individual have the required professional working environment?

If you find the answer to any of these questions is "no," then you and/or someone in the supervisory chain bear some portion of the responsibility for failure. Remember that creating an environment for success is your job and it is your responsibility to fix the problem. If the answers to all of these questions are "yes," then you need to hold the individual accountable and take appropriate action.

Look at your discipline process as a unique opportunity for mentoring subordinates in a very personal setting. By making the process as inclusive as possible without denying the individual appropriate privacy, you will have an opportunity to meet with airmen and NCOs in private settings and teach them your philosophy of leadership. Most disciplinary situations, including those that involve the judge advocate general (JAG), should involve an individual's entire chain of supervision.

Your first step will be to gather together as many facts as possible. Rarely will you have to make split-second decisions in cases of discipline. Be patient and get all of the facts before you take any action. Not only will this ensure that you act based on the best information available, it will also help you avoid an unfair decision when emotions are high. Your first sergeant will be the best resource for finding facts in most cases.

With as many facts as possible on the table, study the information until you can walk through the case chronologically in your mind. Work with the first sergeant to ensure you understand all the intricacies involved. Realize, however, that you will seldom get all of the facts. You just need to be able to walk through the chronology of events in order to form an initial opinion on which way to proceed. Keep this opinion between you and your shirt.

Generally, the next decision you must make is the appropriate level to handle the problem. As a general rule, pushing discipline down to the lowest possible level is advisable. When an airman walks into the commander's office for discipline, it should be a significant emotional event. Ensure that the cases you handle are appropriate for commander involvement. With the exception of officers that work directly for you, any discipline below a letter of reprimand (LOR) should be handled at a lower level. If you choose to handle every case, even in small squadrons, you not only demean the appropriate authority of your office, you also deny subordinate supervisors the opportunity to lead. In cases where you can delegate the disciplinary responsibility, serve as an advisor and mentor to the subordinate supervisor as he or she handles the case.

Once a situation is deemed appropriate for your direct oversight and involvement, call in the leadership chain of the individual—everyone from his or her immediate supervisor through the chief, flight commander, and so forth. As you work through this case, one of your objectives is to mentor everyone in the room. At the first meeting, lay out the facts—from memory, if possible. It will be immediately apparent that you've done your homework and you understand the specifics. If the case involves a young airman, the senior airman and staff sergeant supervisors will see that you take discipline seriously—and this information will get into the squadron quickly.

Once the chronological facts of the case have been reviewed, explain to all that the purpose of this meeting is for you to hear their thoughts on the case and get their answer to a single crucial question: *Is this individual a keeper or not?* Make a solemn point that you carry two tool bags. One is labeled "*rehabilitation*," the other "*removal from the Air Force.*" Before any steps are taken, you need their honest assessment and advice as to which tool bag to open. Make a point that you take their comments seriously and want to know if they are prepared to continue to work with the individual in question. Start with the lowest ranking member present and work up the chain (note: do not go in reverse if you want the senior airman to speak openly). Let everyone speak his or her piece. Pay close attention to the lowest ranking supervisor. Not only does he/she know the individual best, it may be the first time they have been faced with a supervisory issue. Remember, as you work toward a fair discipline solution, that you are using this opportunity to teach. Keep the meeting disciplined and serious. Cut off any and all inappropriate levity among the supervisors present. Joking about the case will undermine your intent and give the impression that the process is more show than substance. Take your own notes as everyone comments, but do not agree or disagree with anyone in the room. Ask questions intended solely to ensure that you understand clearly the position of the individual speaking. Finally, keep the meeting focused on the individual and the case. Cut off any sidebar or conversation that veer from your intended purpose. When everyone has spoken, refer to your notes and summarize each person's viewpoint. Again, begin with the lowest ranking member and spend the most time on his or her comments—you want everyone in the room to know that you value their opinion and take their role as supervisor seriously.

The next step is a gut check. If there is clear consensus in the room on the general way ahead and this consensus agrees with your initial opinion (your "gut"), you might choose to summarize and move to the next step. If the consensus is for dismissal from the Air Force, there is little more for the group to discuss. Tell those present you intend to include them in the rest of the process, yet the final decision will be yours to make. This is a responsibility of command and one you accept and welcome freely.

Chances are, you already have a military lawyer (JAG) assigned to assist your squadron, and the shirt has probably been in contact with him or her. In working with the JAG, the best advice to remember throughout is as follows: *Lawyers are responsible for the law, but commanders are responsible for justice.* I have found military lawyers to be professionals who try their best to give sound legal advice. However, I never went to the JAG and asked, "What do I do?" Rather, I went to the JAG with an idea already thought through with my shirt and key supervisors and asked, "How do I accomplish this plan legally and ethically?" With a plan already in mind, you will find the JAG to be helpful in ensuring that you execute your commander's intent in accordance with military law. If, on the other hand, you ask the JAG to determine the proper way to handle a case, you will get sound legal advice, but it may not achieve justice for your airman. When you are removing an individual from the Air Force, the JAG and your first sergeant will be critical assets.

If the consensus (including your gut feel) is clearly for rehabilitation, you may choose to open the floor for discussion on the tools available in the rehabilitation tool bag. A primary purpose is to teach everyone in the room your process for determining punishment that is just and appropriate. Lay out the intent and procedures for Letters of Counseling, Admonishment, Reprimand, and Article 15. As a new commander, you may feel more comfortable allowing your shirt or the JAG to cover the details of these tools. Believe me, it won't be long before you will be very comfortable covering them yourself.

Once the procedural rules have been covered, go around the room again and ask for opinions on what tool each believes would be appropriate. Same as before—lowest ranking to highest, take notes, offer no opinions, listen actively, and summarize their opinions at the end. Try to determine the best approach to take in assisting this individual back onto the road to success—the purpose of this tool bag. One method for gauging the true mood of the group is to ask for opinions on possible additional duty. If the interest is truly on rehabilitation, the focus will be on structuring the time to retrain the individual in the area(s) where he or she fell short. If the discussion veers towards punitive use of this time, you may be in the wrong tool bag.

Ensure that the supervisors in the room remain personally involved, no matter which package you ultimately choose. If that package is rehabilitation, they must remain personally involved throughout the rehabilitative process. Your ultimate long-term goal is to get this airman back on track. Achieving this goal will require the support of everyone in the room. Once you are satisfied they understand their role in the process, end the meeting with a reminder that all discussions relative to the specifics of the case are to remain within the group.

After you dismiss the supervisors, give a copy of your notes to your first sergeant and ask him or her to summarize them in a "memo for record" for inclusion in the case file. Your shirt will be ultimately responsible for ensuring that the paperwork is correct. Keeping accurate notes throughout will help immensely if any problems occur down the road.

Now it's time to determine where you want to go with the discipline package. Avoid making a quick decision, even if you know exactly what you want to do. Sleep on it one night, not only to review your notes and think over what you have heard but also to avoid the appearance of quickly disregarding the opinion of the supervisors. Once you have made your decision, go over the details with your first sergeant, chief, and/or JAG to minimize the chances that unintended consequences (personnel actions, family repercussions, financial hardship) will occur.

Call the key supervisors back in to tell them your decision. This can be a smaller group but should, at the least, include the people who will be responsible for the rehabilitative program. While you owe no one an explanation of your reasoning, I would advise you to go over the logic you used to come to your decision. Doing so will shed light on your depth as a commander and will allow you to mentor and teach subordinates as you prepare them for greater leadership responsibilities. Use this meeting to dictate the time for delivering the punishment to the offender. Once again, advise them to keep all details of this discussion within the group.

There is certainly no "approved solution" for administering punishment. Much of how you handle this final part of the discipline process will depend on your personality and style. However, here are a few thoughts on effectively ensuring that you achieve your goal.

Being disciplined by the commander should be a significant emotional event. You want every airman in your squadron to dread standing on your carpet. The individual's supervisors should show up five to 10 minutes early and stand in the room in a military manner. Ensure that all present understand the solemnity and importance of this session. You must tailor your delivery to ensure that the message is concise, serious, formal, and *professional.* Make no mistake: You have no right to be abusive. Clear your desk of all but the punishment you are passing out—nothing else should be on your mind while the offender is in the room. Ensure that the shirt pre-briefs the offender on proper reporting procedures as he marches into the office. Once he reports in, keep him at attention and direct that he look at you. Much of what you say is going to be lost on him, but he will remember the direct eye contact. You must prepare before the session so that you can maintain eye contact with minimal referral to your notes. It is acceptable to have your shirt read the fine print for the first few sessions until you become more familiar with the wording. You do not want to get into any discussion at this point. This is truly intended to be a one-sided conversation. If the tool bag you chose is removal, end the session and have the individual report to the first sergeant's office. There, the shirt should go over the details of the package in a more relaxed environment in order to ensure that the airman clearly understands the details of the path you have chosen.

If the tool you chose is rehabilitation, you will find it very effective to order the individual to turn and look at his supervisors at the end. You should then say, "the reason this rehabilitative disciplinary package was chosen is primarily because the leaders you are looking at honestly believe you have the potential to overcome this event and succeed in our Air Force. They are committed to working with you to get you back on track. That being said, none are willing to carry you. We will provide you with the opportunity—it is your job to seize it." Avoid any two-way conversation and dismiss the individual to the shirt's office for follow-up counseling.

You will find that handling discipline will take up a good portion of your time and energy; it is critical that you get it right. While the methods I suggested do not constitute "the approved solution," they do serve as a starting point to develop what works for you. The best description of the process I laid out is "tough love." Remember two critical items:

1. Develop your process as an opportunity to mentor—make it inclusive.

2. In the end, discipline handled fairly is always good and you alone are ultimately responsible for justice.

This chapter will conclude with a couple of stories from commanders who faced difficult disciplinary situations. To protect the privacy of all parties, no names or bases are mentioned.

I had a technical sergeant in the squadron who tested positive on a random urinalysis test a couple days after Christmas. Everyone, including me, could not believe he would use marijuana. Nonetheless, the JAG informed me that we must take the case to court-martial because he was an NCO and I had no say in the matter.

Three months elapsed as prosecution made its case and waited for trial. The defense attorney prepared an active defense, showing that a level of THC [tetrahydrocannabinol] in one's system could be caused by ingestion of hemp seed oil. This was backed up by scientific evidence that even a teaspoon-size amount of this product will trigger the test. His results were at an extremely low level—barely enough to flag the test and conducive to the argument. Additionally, the technical sergeant claimed he had been to a friend's home for dinner on the night before the test where hemp seed oil was indeed used by the hostess. Both the hostess and her husband filed affidavits to this effect.

The technical sergeant had over forty character references from a variety of people, including the logistics group commander and the top chief master sergeant from our Numbered Air Force.

A couple days before the scheduled court-martial, the JAG came to me with a "deal" they wanted to offer the technical sergeant—bad conduct discharge in lieu of court-martial. He would avoid a felony conviction but be forced to give up a sixteen-year career and have to live with the discharge on his permanent records.

The entire case came back to me because I would have to enforce the discharge. I asked if I could dismiss the case and was told yes, but any commander above me could void the dismissal and send the case directly to trial. If this were to happen, the "deal" would be voided and result in a rather large risk for the sergeant. His attorneys believed the case sat at fifty-fifty for conviction.

I discussed all of the options with the technical sergeant, along with his wife and his counsel, reminding him that he could accept the deal, or that I could take the matter for my consideration and either send it to court, discharge him, or dismiss the case. After counsel with his attorney, he elected to let my decision be the final word.

After more than a week to review the case, re-reading all of the evidence presented, I determined that enough reasonable doubt existed to suggest that the defense had made its case. It was an agonizing decision. I did not want to be over-ridden and have this young man face a felony conviction when he could have left with a bad conduct discharge. Happily for the young man, none of the commanders above me reversed the decision. I am confident I made the right decision and the most just outcome was achieved.

The final story involves an extremely tough situation: The commander had to balance doing what he thought was right with achieving a timely outcome to a difficult case. You may face a case in which the cost of pursuing it is too high a price for the unit to pay. There is *not* a "right" answer in a case like this. Think about how you would have handled the situation.

As I took command, I inherited a few discipline situations that were already underway. One involved·an office of special investigation (OSI) case against a senior airman who was just months away from a discharge for high-year tenure. The investigation revealed that the senior airman, while stationed previously overseas, had sexual relations several times with a minor. As the investigation came to a close, it became clear that to get a court-martial conviction, we would need testimony from the minor involved.

She was a dependent of a retired master sergeant, still living overseas, who had refused permission to fly her back for testimony in the case. As such, the JAG informed me there was no way to win a case against the airman. I chose to approach the wing commander and ask for funds to fly a legal team overseas to gain the testimony. The wing commander agreed.

However, the JAG felt that even with a written statement, we only had a marginal chance for conviction. I asked the JAG to contact the area defense counsel (ADC) and inform him that we not only were intent on gaining the testimony from the minor but we were also prepared to prosecute to the maximum extent possible.

In less than a day, the ADC came back with a deal. He proposed that they seek discharge in lieu of court-martial which would result in him being out of the Air Force in 3 days, a lifelong discharge statement that read "in lieu of court-martial," and loss of his high year tenure separation pay (about $22,000). I opted to allow the discharge and we got him out of the Air Force as quickly as possible.

Unfortunately, the story doesn't end there. Approximately a year after the discharge, the SrA killed his own daughter and then killed himself during a shootout with police. The question I will forever face is, what would have happened if I had been able to gain a conviction and send him to prison?

A final thought on handling discipline within the squadron: You must follow up. Once a case is deemed appropriate for your involvement as commander, you should insist on receiving updates on the process to ensure that the intended outcome is being achieved. The updates will not only confirm that your intent is being carried out, it will give you one more opportunity to interact with the individual's supervisory chain in a mentoring forum.

# Chapter 5

# **Great Ideas**

*Choose work you love and you will never have to work a day in your life.*

—Confucius

*Good thoughts in your head not delivered mean squat.*

—Kenneth Blanchard

The purpose of this chapter is to offer you some program ideas to ponder as you mentally prepare for command. While far from all-inclusive, they are intended to spark your imagination as you develop your own programs for success. Once again, these thoughts come from across the Air Force and, as such, have been ops-tested in the field by the commanders interviewed.

## **Take Responsibility for *Fun***

By taking responsibility for *fun* in your squadron, you will not only improve morale, you will produce memories that will endure long after your command tour ends. People in your organization should *want* to have your job. Not because of all the responsibility it entails or because of the power or prestige. They should want to be a commander someday because it looks like you are having so much darn fun in the job. Believe me, this is far easier said than done. As you have seen in many of the stories shared thus far, there will be plenty of moments when the job will seem overwhelming and at times no fun at all. Keep these thoughts to yourself or your peers. An enthusiastic commander radiates his or her enthusiasm throughout the squadron. It is a timeproven truth that squadrons take on the personality of the commander over time—warts and all. If you are a grump, your squadron will generally not be a happy place to work. People will key on your mood. Walk in and slam the door to your office some day. Within 10 minutes, many folks in your squadron will know that something is up and many key supervisors will waste valuable time wondering whether they did something to put you in such a foul mood. By the end of the day, your mood will be reflected across the squadron.

We often don't realize the effect we have on our units as "the boss." Be positive and enthusiastic about your squadron, your mission, and your role as commander. On the other hand, I would never advise putting on a show. Unless you've had some serious acting training, your troops will see through you in a second and you will have the reverse effect. It is not necessary to be positive every minute of every day. At times, you might need to show some carefully controlled anger to ensure appropriate emphasis is placed on a problem area. However, in general, you must work to be a positive influence on the squadron.

Lt Col Dave "Face" Nichols is among the most positive commanders I've worked with. At Aviano AB, Italy, his enthusiasm and love of the 510th Fighter Squadron, the Buzzards, resonated around the wing. He agreed to share a few words on leadership with us.

People make leadership exciting, complex, frustrating, and rewarding. I approach the challenge with a simple acronym—ICE. It stands for intelligence, compassion, energy, and experience. Let me briefly mention each.

*Intelligence* is your learned and studied abilities, your technical competence, and your leadership skills; that is, your bag of knowledge. As the commander, you must understand the technical aspects of your business and be among the best at what you do—this will free you to lead. Don't try to gain this "intelligence" in a vacuum. Learn about your mission and understand your people. Know what they and others expect of the squadron. Let the "smart guys" in the unit help spin you up. Read about and understand other leaders. Never think you have learned it all—continue to study until the day you pass on the unit guidon. Be an intelligent leader.

*Compassion* is easy to explain but very difficult to accomplish. Your people need to know that you care about them and that they can trust you to look out for their interests. I tried to start on the right foot with each new "Buzzard" by insisting that he or she take the first two weeks off after arrival to get their families settled. I encouraged them to spend time at home, then I explained why—it was entirely selfish on my part. While they were assigned as "Buzzards," there would be times when we would have to work long and hard both deployed and at home. We were never more than 24 hours from loading live ordnance on our aircraft and flying them into harms way. I made it clear that when this happened, I needed them focused 100 percent on the job at hand—not worrying about problems at home. I also encouraged them to share their experiences with their loved ones so they would feel part of what we were doing.

Approach your command opportunity with *energy*. Make sure that people know and can see that you are excited about your job as commander. Let them feel and be a part of your excitement—enough so that the workplace becomes energized and enjoyable. Enthusiasm is contagious—spread it wisely.

The final letter in the acronym is hidden—it stands for *experience.* This is something that comes with time in the seat, and it ties the acronym together. Use not only your experience but also others both inside and outside the squadron. No one has all the answers to the often-complex situations you will be faced with as a commander. Tap into as many sources as possible and avoid "going it alone" on the tough ones. Chances are, someone around you has faced a similar situation and can offer helpful advice.

Remember that you have been chosen to command because of your demonstrated success. Leadership will be a daily challenge for you as a commander. Use the ICE acronym to help. More than anything though, enjoy every minute—it truly is the best job in the Air Force![1]

## Sponsor Program

Of all the "people" programs you will have in your squadron, none is more critical to the long-term health of the squadron than the sponsor program. The positive benefits are immeasurable. When a new member of your squadron arrives, have the sponsor gather as many folks as possible, throw on your squadron T-shirts and ball caps, and go meet the family. Often they arrive tired and beat from a long trip. Find a local restaurant that is willing to adopt your squadron and hang your patch on the wall. Make this the location you frequent for incoming family dinners. Obviously, you can't make every dinner. However, you should establish a process during your weekly staff meeting that informs you of incoming personnel and sponsor assignment. Establish a standard procedure to ensure that the sponsor is allowed time off to help the new family get settled. Encourage spouse support groups to get involved in the welcome. Dazzle the newcomers with a sense of family—they are joining an elite unit that takes care of each other. Your personal interest in the program will resonate around the squadron. Talk about the program at monthly commander's calls. Follow up during monthly newcomer briefings. If you learn that a squadron member arrived with no sponsorship, find out what happened. Again, the positive payback of this program is immeasurable. Not only is it fun, it becomes perpetual. When it becomes this family's turn to sponsor a new member, they know how the game is played. In the Air Force, we recruit individuals but we retain families. When someone in your squadron comes upon the inevitable decision point of whether to remain in the Air Force or move on to civilian life, you want them to weigh the "fun factor" in their decision. We cannot compete with the commercial sector in the salary or stability game. What we do have to offer is service that makes a difference and unmatched camaraderie anywhere on the globe. You want your troops to know that the treatment they received when they arrived in your squadron will never be repeated at Delta Airlines or Microsoft. This kind of family environment and support network only exists in our Air Force. It is your job to make this a priority and to train the next group of commanders to continue the tradition.

# Celebrate Heroes—
# Not Machines

Research and celebrate the proud history of your unit. If you don't have a squadron historian, hire one within. Have him or her research through the Air University or the Air Force Historian the places and times your unit has been called for duty. Before you take command (or as soon as possible thereafter), study the squadron's history. You are joining a potentially long line of former commanders who gave their heart and soul to the unit you now command. Get in touch with them. Ask for their assistance in bringing the history of the squadron to life. Invite them to the squadron for a commander's call. If you are lucky enough to live in proximity with past squadron members, invite them out and make them feel part of today's squadron. How many units in the Air Force can you walk into today that celebrate their proud history throughout their facilities? Chances are, most squadrons you have been in have celebrated machines rather than heroes. Specifically, we tend to put pictures of aircraft all around our squadrons but do little to honor the men and women who wore your squadron patch in previous years. We need to reverse this trend across our Air Force and you can begin with your squadron. The benefit will be quickly seen as members realize they are part of a long line of professionals who have been in your unit. By developing an association with those who've "gone before," you bring this history to life.

## Mentoring Program

As a commander, one of your key roles is to teach—to develop those entrusted to your care to their fullest potential and prepare them for future leadership challenges. While you are putting out the inevitable daily fires, you can easily neglect this responsibility. When Col Lansen Conley commanded the maintenance squadron at Aviano, he developed a superb mentoring program:

After becoming a squadron commander, I found myself in some sense unprepared for the job. Sure I attended the squadron commander's course and got all the hot tips from previous commanders. But commanding is more than just knowledge. It is knowing how and what to think about, how to correctly apply the knowledge you have (wisdom), and understanding the real role of the commander. These things are only learned over time. I decided, therefore, that one of my jobs as commander was to prepare my younger officers for future command. As such, I set up a function called "Hoofers and Doofers" for mentoring. Once a month I assigned one of my officers to host the function, usually Friday afternoon around 1600. The host officer would provide a room with food and drinks. When we met, in an informal atmosphere, I would present the officers with a real world situation I was dealing with or had just dealt with, and let each discuss it and provide a recommendation. Once the discussion was complete, I would offer my insights and tell them what I did and why. I also used the time to listen to what was on their minds—good and bad. This was a great forum for helping them develop their "sense of the commander." They were eager to attend and enjoyed participating as much as I did.[2]

Clearly, there are an infinite number of great ideas for improving the quality of service and quality of life for your airmen. For any program to succeed and become self-sufficient, it must have three critical ingredients:

1. A single person in charge who is accountable

2. A carefully studied and executable plan

3. A plan for follow-up to track success[3]

When a program fails, look back and you will likely find that one of these three items is missing. Most often, we tend to get the first two accomplished but fail to follow up appropriately. Develop a systematic approach that allows you to keep focused on a wide array of programs in the squadron to ensure that they stay on track.

Remember that any program you initiate should fit into a broader plan, which you developed when you laid out your vision. By following these basic rules, you will be well on your way to establishing viable and exciting programs that will survive long past the day you give up the squadron.

**A team of dedicated military professionals makes your Air Force squadron go.**

## Notes

1. Col Dave Nichols, USAF, interviewed by author, February 2001.

2. Col Lansen Conley, USAF, interviewed by author, January 2001.

3. Gen Mike Ryan, USAF, interviewed by author, June 1996.

# Conclusion

*It is truly an honor to be selected to command in the US Air Force. Your challenge is to be worthy of that honor.*

—Gen John P. Jumper

The reality of the present and near future is clear. We will be called upon to utilize aerospace power around the world more frequently in support of national security objectives. By nature of the medium we exploit, the technology at our disposal, and the demonstrated professionalism of our airmen, we in the Air Force are best able to project military power around the world without projecting corresponding vulnerability. Whether we like it or not, we are the low risk option in the national security tool bag for both coercive and decisive warfare. Accomplishing these missions, at the level of expertise and professionalism our nation has come to expect, takes preparation, innovation, courage, and absolute adherence to our core values. As a squadron commander, you are essential to achieving this success. If reading this paper has helped you mentally prepare for duty and given you "*food for thought*" as you ponder how you want to command your squadron, I will have accomplished my objective. Best of luck and clear skies in the best job you will ever have!

# Bibliography

Air University (AU)-2, *Guidelines for Command.* Air Command and Staff College (ACSC). Maxwell Air Force Base (AFB), Ala.: Air University Press, 1995.

Blanchard, Kenneth H. *The Heart of a Leader.* Tulsa, Okla.: Honor Books, 1999.

Coles, Robert. *Lives of Moral Leadership.* New York: Random House, 2000.

Gergen, David R. *Eyewitness to Power: The Essence of Leadership: Nixon to Clinton.* New York: Simon & Schuster, 2000.

Ledeen, Michael A. *Machiavelli on Modern Leadership: Why Machiavelli's Iron Rules Are As Timely and Important Today As Five Centuries Ago.* New York: Truman Talley Books, 1999.

Lester, Richard I., PhD, ed. AU-24, *Concepts for Air Force Leadership.* Maxwell AFB, Ala.: Air University Press, 1990.

Meyer, John G., Maj Gen, USA. *Company Command: The Bottom Line.*

Alexandria, Va.: Byrrd Enterprises, 1996.

Perkins, Dennis N. T. *Leading at the Edge: Leadership Lessons from the Extraordinary Saga of Shackleton's Antarctic Expedition.* New York: Amacom, 2000.

Smith, Perry M. *Rules & Tools for Leaders.* Garden City Park, N.Y.: Avery Publishing Group, 1998.

Stockdale, Jim and Sybil. *In Love and War: The Story of a Family's Ordeal and Sacrifice During the Vietnam Years.* Annapolis, Md.: Naval Institute Press, 1990.

Timmons, Timothy T., Col, USAF. *Commanding an Air Force Squadron.* Maxwell AFB, Ala.: Air University Press, 1993.

# Index